William F. DeVault

Selected Poems and Passions: 1972-1996

William F. DeVault

Selected Poems and Passions: 1972-1996

Other books by William F. DeVault include

PanthEon	ISBN #0-9659576-0-8
From an Unexpected Quarter	ISBN #0-5950023-1-5
Love Gods of a Forgotten Religion	ISBN #0-5952225-2-8
101 Great Love Poems (Hardbound)	ISBN #0-5956540-2-9
101 Great Love Poems (Softbound)	ISBN #0-5952588-2-4
INVOCATO	ISBN #1-4116293-1-0
THE COMPLEAT PANTHER CYCLES	ISBN #1-4116379-4-1
The Morgantown Suite Poems	ISBN #1-4116337-4-1
Ronin in the Temple of Aphrodite	ISBN #978-1-4303-0425-8
Psalms of the Monster River Cult (co-authored with Daniel S. McTaggart)	ISBN #978-1-4357-0728-3
As such…	ISBN #978-1-4357-1448-9
loveaddict	ISBN #978-0-557-28390-3
Selected Poems and Passions: 2004-2011	ISBN #978-0-615-54937-8
Selected Poems and Passions: 1996-2004	ISBN #978-1-478-17676-3

Selected Poems and Passions: 1972-1996
© William F. DeVault

Published by Apokalypsis   www.cityoflegends.com
ISBN:

No part of this book may be reproduced or transmitted in any form or by any means, graphic, electronic, or mechanical, including photocopying, recording, taping, or by any information storage or retrieval system, without permission in writing from the publisher.

William F. DeVault

To the past,
        To the present,
                To the future,

            And all who dwell there.

William F. DeVault

A brief word from the author

I could have taken this book all the way back to 1963 and my first poem, "O, Ship!" but decided adding a decade just to snag one poem (most of the rest of that decade was dreck) made no sense.

So I decided to start with my earliest romantic works and play up until 1996, crossing over into the Panther era. Note that I have included "The Goldenheart Cycles" as part of this package. And, I think, overall, we lay some groundwork for a quick base for my future works.

Evolving through romantic and metaphysical influences, and including some of my more interesting and durable works (which is somewhat unfair, as older works would automatically be seen as more durable) we have a buffet of influences and styles as I sought to find and refine my voice.

My thanks to cover model Ifigenia, who captures the leggy intensity of Psyche, one of my first totem-muses, who inspired many of my earliest surviving works. Had I met her back then, who knows what my path would have been. And also to my constant collaborator, Mariya Andriichuk, whose image illuminates this manuscript in a few select points.

Be well, be strong, and enjoy.

William F. DeVault

Selected Poems and Passions: 1972-1996

Monument	1
The Unicorns	2
couplet/passion	3
tread softly	4
I should have been immortal	5
to the dark maiden of sorrows	6
a locked instant in the stream of time	7
Satin Scars	8
Unborn Years	9
Bragi bleeds	10
a dark liqueur	11
gibbous	12
memory of a blindman's illusion	13
yesterdays	14
sanctuary	15
tread softly	16
my electric lady	17
penance	18
the sorrow of past errors	19
last night	20
the faceted sphere: one	21
Charlotte's song	22
Virgin's dawn	23
the lingering haste	24
Nemicorn	25
alien gods	26
leper's blood	27
horizon	28
the faceted sphere: 27	29
the faceted sphere: 28	30
You asked for It (when Peri complains)	31
The Amomancer Dances in the Shadows	32
The Goldenheart Cycles	33
Cycle One: Innocence	34
the feathers of the phoenix	35
the sand castles	35
wind of gold and jasmine	36
iron box	37
the flavour of time	37
the gypsy moth	38

  mirror within my mind 38
Cycle Two: Invocation 39
  a taste of brimstone 40
  soft arms 40
  homeless heart 41
  Edward bares his soul 41
  The taste of blood 42
  softer than skin 42
  eternal kiss 42
Cycle Three: Memory's Shores 43
  venom of time 44
  glycerin tears 44
  a world of challenges 45
  the gem of fire 45
  goldenheart by twilight 46
  bracing for Ragnarok 47
  autumnal 47
Cycle Four: Dreams of the Damned 48
  nightmare 49
  wet dream 49
  dream of falling 50
  the second nightmare 50
  waking dream 51
  sleepwalker 51
  daydream 52
Cycle Five: the Cold Illusions 53
  second chances 54
  virtue and vice 54
  a little warmth 54
  bartering truth 55
  golden hearts by the pound 55
  reflections on a wind forced by the passage of time 56
  leap of faith 56
Cycle Six: the Delta 57
  soft 58
  warm 58
  willing 59
  wet 59
  gentle feast 60
  chosen voices 60
  impalement 61

Cycle Seven: Consummation and Beyond 62
    commitment 63
    ancient skies 63
    new life 64
    the peasant blouse 64
    security 65
    the centaur's home in a golden heart 65
    bare feet on a wooden floor 66
About the author 67

William F. DeVault

Monument

I crave a cup. a bowl. a mug of your heart's steel.
unsheathed before by mortal or god for rage or lust
of things both unneeded and forever unreal...
it is the quintessence...and the dust.

dreams do not stand before you and call the blade.
dreams do not walk or breathe or love you as I do.
and can. and will, if given just a moment's shade
from the moon of pain and the stars that lie.

my words shall be eternal. syntax monuments of you.
beneath the tread of centuries, stone shall fall.
paint peel. music rise to ears long deaf. but now...
and from this night on...you are immortal.

The Unicorns

Please come awhile, remain and play.
The unicorns won't come today.
The faeries and their virtued kin
shall stay away, to paint my sin.
with ancient red and angry fire.

Please come to me and linger, please.
I do not mock, I dare not tease.
Just bring with you an honest smile
and share with me, for all the while,
a love of life and true desire.

The unicorns no longer guard
the meadow just beyond my yard.
They snort with shame and true disdain
upon a hope of ages' pain
and brand me, by their pride, a liar.

couplet/passion

if my passion is my poison, then better still to die
as the victim of the vineyard than the champion of a lie.

tread softly

tread softly on the carpets of my soul.
before no other have they been laid, so open,
and were they to be abused...surely I would die.
weave carefully your dreams to make me whole.
fashion them discreetly, do not parade
my love for you like some new toy...before every eye.
carve my flesh with blades of trust.
fear not my death, for I am made strong
by the love I sense in you...a love I know we share.
bury me not beneath time's dust,
for memory lies and I will live long
and at peace within the world...as only lovers may dare.

I should have been immortal

lying in fields of orchids, I dream of roses.
there is not...there will not be...
there can not be enough time to taste
all the wines. I should have been immortal.

the wind blows warm when I crave the ice.
the pie is cut. but I want no slice
of it...yet the cake I need
has been served all around.

I have sailed the sun and touched the moon and
fallen to earth in death's calling...but where
are the ancients...I must know. I will go to see
their tombs...for I am too late
(or they passed too soon).
their's will be my destiny, too...to dream
of fires that shall not burn in my earthtime...
to carve my name on a sapling and not live to see
the process spread my words to gargantuan proportions...

yet, security beckons. there is
a sort of pleasure in knowing that
death waits around a farther hill, and that
you will be blessed by its frostbound visitation.

but I should have been. I could have been. I would
have been immortal. there just isn't enough
time for the roses.

to the dark maiden of sorrows

you are dark,
an ebon ribbon
that has twined about my soul.
you are black,
a burning chestwound
playing passion in control
of memory,
both remembered
and dreamt in troubling sleep
where the dreams are moist, electric,
and in shadows brittly creep.

you are light,
yet undiscovered
in your incandescent prayers.
you are flame
that licks the tapers
casting light in devils' lairs.

you are blood
and resolution
and questions I won't ask
out of fear
that the answers
might prove a poisoned cask
of the wine
of your passions
barely seen in sacred night
but I must
if I wish to
be the one who burns your light

you are light,
yet undiscovered
in your incandescent prayers.
you are flame
that licks the tapers
casting light in devils' lairs.

William F. DeVault

a locked instant in the stream of time

and when at last passes this iota of remorse
for illusions held in fond remembrance,
do not judge too harshly the flow and course
of a sickly heart. do not acknowledge a chance
to taste the amber fruit that dangles so
unappetizingly before you, for the fire burns
deep valleys in the flesh and soul to show
to all the folly of a fool's desire as turns
a thought unspoken to the sun. cold shades
and blind parades of time we'll never share
within a lost moment. silence serenades
us for a moment. then I avert my eyes.

Satin Scars

like satin scars on scaly skin,
my words exceed me.
memory fails and I am transient...
but my soul can see beyond
the farthest thunder of the
birth of time. the dance proceeds
at such a speed I cannot end the crime.
for all my cunning and fire,
I am a frail mortal. I bend
in the wind and cry in the dark
and withdraw, a bloodied friend betrayed
by self and shame, the game contorts
and fades. it laughs a Manson laugh...
in the face of the decades.
the decades that rob me,
that raped you and stole my god.
the dance I once began...I cannot begin
to prod my mind for the simplest steps..
memory fails and I am a cipher.
a riddle that no one laughs at,
a purpose none would die for.
but even in the grayest light I find
the answer. the time was not for me...
I stole it out of love and fear,
a crime so hideous...but so human.
there is much to forget and forgive,
to deny that is to lie.
and yet, for all our sins, we live.

Unborn Years

and the silent, sentient shadow of silence shall fall
over a sad seeming dream, woven of gossamer and cold tears
shed in precognitive memory of times that never shall
belong to me. times that suffered in the greyness of unborn years.

Bragi bleeds

the serpent and the succubus
are baring polished fang for you.
I caught the faintest glimmer
of greylight off their
ruby-blue metal surfaces.
I heard the sheaths' whispering
to me again last night
as I dreamed memory.

slow cuts the quickslitter
that drives home venom angry
and opaque. take this phial
and drink warm wine tonight
when they come for you, as I do.
no less breathes a riddle than I.
no more to dream
the clocks' mockery.

a dark liqueur

and through cool and cruel vermilion lips
the web is woven. the huntress sips
a dark liqueur. paradise and paradox,
the shadow forms only with light and walks
away, dissolving in the dark. to taste
the softness with a hunger not in haste
but in reverence and focused passion held
and commanded by a mind set against a legion swelled.

gibbous

the shameless moon, illuminating all
the sins I imagined with you.
scheming, dreaming of the frail silk
made window to the touch of my eyes
as you crossed the room into my arms.
into my soul.
into my night.
and I thanked the moon
for the pale blue curve of your breasts.

memory of a blindman's illusion

the reds and golds had melted down to flow across the grays...
you asked me for an answer to the riddle I'd once told.
the blues and fecund violets were counting all the days...
the puzzle pondered Plato, though he knew the trail was cold.

the cigarette was bitter, but the taste was all the same.
I asked a dark reflection if he knew me by my name.
the glass I drained, it lay there...just feeding on the dregs.
the goblet's handle felt to be the image of your legs.

a thousand shades of ebony descended with a laugh...
the bloodstains on my forehead now asked for a cup of tea.
the silvers and the cobalts now killed the sacred calf.
the auctioneer recanted and my soul was sold for free.

every woman dressed in red had slept with me before.
and every woman dressed in black lay dying on the floor.
the reptile lady danced for you...she climaxed with a yawn.
we drank the lies and told the wine until the early dawn.

yesterdays

learn to live with your regrets.
swallow your pride and carry inside
all the crosses you have made.
cry, just once, for all the yesterdays.
steel against the fears of the mockery of the tears
and be thankful for having seen the passed parade.

sanctuary

in darkness...
an all-pervasive silence to the eyes,
dotted only by distant gleaming jewels
of hydrogen infernos...
their sanctuary so far
that I could not walk to them
in a million sleepless lifetimes.
so alone...
looking forward to see no cities
or nations or worlds bearing life,
or even an honest promise of it.
I strain with metal ears
to catch the faintest whisper
that never comes...just silence.
to heavens
I reach with open heart
and a prayer of a hope of a dream
of a chance that there is someone there...
someone who hears me...
and is willing to share a dream...
a dream of a destiny beyond Thulcandra.

tread softly

tread softly on the carpets of my soul.
before no other have they been laid, so open,
and were they to be abused...surely I would die.
weave carefully your dreams to make me whole.
fashion them discreetly, do not parade
my love for you like some new toy...before every eye.
carve my flesh with blades of trust.
fear not my death, for I am made strong
by the love I sense in you...a love I know we share.
bury me not beneath time's dust,
for memory lies and I will live long
and at peace within the world...as only lovers may dare.

my electric lady

dance for me, my electric lady.
sing a song that gently soothes my soul.
tomorrow I must leave your world again, my love...
as I strive to reach this endless journey's goal.

I once gave up my poor and mortal birthright,
so that I might touch the sky and see true things.
my love, I'm not so sure I would have started,
if I could have seen the pain this voyage brings.

once again, my electric lady,
touch me and bring forth my too-rare smile.
for the moment I am just another mortal-
and a little love will last me quite a while.

if we had only met before the present,
and what is gone had made me what I am,
a love would be that all who live might envy-
but I cannot come back this way again.

for the final time, my electric lady...
give me all that I may take within my vow.
tomorrow is my child and a gift to the stars-
and the night is just my brother here and now.

penance

against the odds
against the gods forced on us
by friend or foe, we fight.
beyond mere will,
where weapons kill more than
just flesh, slaying truth and light.

we have been cast, as tumbling dice,
amidst the mortals who repel us...
who would sell us for a smile
from cold idols carved of ice.
we have fallen. and have risen.
and taken penance given, every mile.

William F. DeVault

the sorrow of past errors

I take my chances and taste the fruits
to see if they are bitter or sweet.
And though they prove bitter
for this am I wiser than those who never did eat.

But how I envy the gifted ones
who can tell with a single glance
if the fruit is poison or richer than honey
and never need take my chance.

last night

you cannot go back.
last night is now dead.
and all that remains
are the stains on the bed.

do not seek excuses.
we all find regret.
it is part of our being,
like blood, spit and sweat.

and just as fluidic.
transient and moist.
evaporated pleasures
we deny were our choice.

though often I regret things,
curses cast at time
may wash away the bloodstains,
but never change the crime.

the faceted sphere: one

the comfort of your kiss. so innocent
that unicorns could watch without grief.
so tempting that, for a moment, a brief
aroma of brimstone flirted with my senses.
there is mystery here, mystery and madness
that begs me to hide from the call of questions
best left unanswered and unasked...veiled confessions
that carry within themselves passion and sadness.
an ending without a beginning...an embrace shared
by lovers in an alternate reality passes by.
and beyond.
the riddle smiles at us and we smile coyly at bonds
that cannot hold us in this sphere...
dreams and nightmares undared.

Charlotte's song

you never need answer the past...
the questions it may ask are meaningless
when the next sun rises and the yesterdays
fall beneath the tread of the tomorrows.
don't sell your soul for riddles...
for answers are what you need--far more
than a puzzled pause of confusion or
the look of silent embarrassment's sorrows.
our destinies once lay on different paths...
but roads have a strange and wonderful way of
merging just beyond the next hill--and now we
glide through life, together, on a single trail.
nothing in this life is truly free...
but you'll find my love freely given
to you in great modesty. it is all I have
to offer. yet, beside it, the sun shall pale.

Virgin's dawn

touch a bitter tear
and run, laughing.
the innocence you prayed to is long gone.
saline reign of fear.
a dream undying.
the wind betrays the come of virgin's dawn.

run a race with fate.
the clocks are melting.
memory is the curse of those who care.
there are those who wait,
their spirits moulding.
our dreams are borne in riddles on the air.

taste the razor snow.
the fire. the beauty.
the dawn is yours, it must be by your choice.
watch our fleshes flow.
feel passions' duty.
your touch and taste shall serve as spirits' voice.

touch a bitter tear
and run, laughing.
the innocence you prayed to is long gone.
saline reign of fear.
a dream undying.
the wind betrays the come of virgin's dawn.

the lingering haste

the warmth. the taste.
the lingering haste that lovers display.
so softly.
so simple. so sweet.
never knowing defeat, you drift away.
so lofty.
gentle and complete.

Nemicorn

...and in my willful innocence I slit the fragile throat
of the Dreamhart, the nemicorn that bore me to my Rubicon.
Its blood, a shaft of crystal whispers, gave amotation
to the feelings I feared, and slew, out of time now gone.

the sniggering empaths capered no more, but lay in pain
among the orchids...crippled by the nemicorn's gentle
acceptance of my treachery and butchery. that placid brain
caring not for a vengeance of the visceral.

Dreamhart knew that time would slay me, time and regret
that would be mine when my all-too mortal form failed
in the icy waters, when I found my strength was set
against powers beyond me. when passion paled.

...and in my willful innocence I slit the fragile throat
of the Dreamhart, the nemicorn that bore me to my Rubicon.
Its blood, a shaft of crystal whispers, gave amotation
to the feelings I feared, and slew, out of time now gone.

alien gods

we pray to them. they prey on us.
they slither back into shadows
at our approach, the better to seize us
unaware to be scrutinized at their leisure.
we give them great pleasure...
we of soft flesh and chewy tendons,
our bones crackling so satisfyingly.
we tempt them. they feed on us.
and we never see them come or go.
we just know that they are out there. waiting.

leper's blood

crimson flows my molten heart with
sorrowed passion.
red, red eyes sealed with wax and amber.
sarcophagus. blind from lust,
for its purpose I live, my mission
and emission programmed for all time.
crush my mind, my soul, my power for the want of release.
evade me, my dreams, that I may wallow in pride
of fleshy memories and members. no peace
for piece, by piece I am undone, cattle ride
their master into the night for an ounce
of satisfaction I cannot have. leper's blood
is all I have to offer as the hot cats pounce
to feast on dry bones of a withered god.
hiding in the light, brittly split and broken,
a token dreamer in a forest of infinity.
iron is my maker, velvet my foil, unspoken
words my epitaph. blood is spilt for sanity.

horizon

there was a season
when I was stronger.
when days lasted longer and wind filled my sails.
there was a reason
for love's trial and error.
ghosts in the mirror were yesterdays' tales.
the winds now are memory.
hope and illusion.
pain and confusion inherit my gold.
but I, I shall live on
the crusts stained with jelly,
filling my belly with morsels and mould.
there is yet a season,
with dragons returning,
the fires yet burning shall lift to the skies.
there must be a reason
to seek the horizons.
to sail for the islands with unclouded eyes.

my sails are of iron. the sun is my shepherd.
and I am the leopard.
the lion. the beast.
alone at the tiller. I seek no more portage.
the winds of an old rage
shall yet drive me east.

the faceted sphere: 27

to touch, for just a fleeting instant, the quintessence
and the antithesis of all I'll ever, never know
but for the laughter of the fate of feeling triumph
in the pain of saline rain bought with riddles and denials.
presence is the mockery. and cruelty is not bought
for a price more precious than sanity,
the vanity of love and lust, again.

the faceted sphere: 28

an etching of an unlikely and improbable and
impossible embrace that is cut into a warm
and plastic mind in honest desire. gentle
and unmocking this imagined unlocking
of the vaults of pleasure in a reality so far from here
that only infinite eyes can pierce the mists of distance and logic.
a puzzle to be prodded as I chase the chaste illusions
of a vision spawned in a single mental image of paradise
consumed for the want of a pauper's measure
of passion and sincere devotion. a whisper
raising fierce illusions of a chance to teach the dance
to an earnest paramour, the price of immortality
the only currency of worth to offer.

You asked for It (when Peri complains)

you asked for a brother. I gave you two.
you didn't complain.
well, the day Elric decide to test
the aerodynamics of fecal matter
didn't play well on your nerves,
but it serves to temper you for your own.

What? you might not have any?
Bull...I've seen the way your eyes light up
reading a book to your brothers.
Or the sideways smirk (you got honestly from me)
right after you've been outraged by their latest abomination
(like the plopping sound in the hall,
investigated
just a second too late).

And you know they love you, too.
The way their eyes light up when they see you.
The way your eyes light up when you see them.

The Amomancer Dances in the Shadows

Can you walk for me softly, like a dream that sheds the night,
to transform the cradled questions in a subtle, steady light?
What colours colding passion, when the palette has gone dry?
What shades our surest evidence, when the premise is a lie?

Who are we to wait in wonder, when the wanderlust returns?
What spell are we fallen under, that lays ashes to our burns?
Can you walk for me softly, like a dream that sheds the night,
to transform the cradled questions in a subtle, steady light?

Can you drink to my memory, when the tantalus runs dry,
leaving dust and rust and lusty crust, our black thirsts to deny?
What use is there for hunger, when the baker's bowl is crushed?
What purpose grows from sacrifice, with the martyr's credo hushed?

When shall we make harvest, when dead husks are all that's sown?
What shall we dare inherit, when our values we disown?
Can you drink to my memory, when the tantalus runs dry,
leaving dust and rust and lusty crust, our black thirsts to deny?

Can you show to me the difference between the streetlights and the sun,
when the darkness in which we bled is shed and the future is begun?
Have you ever dared to drink the dregs of the wine of your own lies?
Have you measured the width of your life's path with only half-open eyes?

Will you teach to me the difference between strong evil and weak fear?
Do you know the test that tells the tale and the tableau of a tear?
Can you show to me the difference between the streetlights and the sun,
when the darkness in which we bled is shed and the future is begun?

The Goldenheart Cycles

Cycle One: Innocence

the feathers of the phoenix

Red. shimmering crimson in the wind.
memories approaching, saints who sinned
in the name of innocence. penance blessed
by a baptism of words. held to a vest
of feathers. bladed shafts of a rare bird,
unique in essence. a fresh flight stirred.

the sand castles

Built by children. sturdy symbols of youth
until the tides of time and tapestry
of maturing emotions and volatile hungers
lay waste the sticky sands. truth
now overturned by the travesty
of evidence and the coming crash of breakers.

wind of gold and jasmine

Standing impassive at the edge of time.
candies for karma. cutting cold for crime
I never intended. my sins invoked.
listening to fools quote words I once spoke.

and there, again. the wind begins, again.
the wind of gold and jasmine, blowing when
it chooses. it loses nothing to time...
it lays the carpets for rhythm and rhyme.

and you are in it. the jasmine carries
the scent of your skin, warm and fresh, buries
senses in an avalanche of desire.
the mist of gold, your image, wakes my fire.

paralyzed by the strong emotions you
create in me. I hate in me this new
arousal. the giant slept for so long
that nothing shall come of his lover's song.

iron box

Victoria kept her secrets.
but you showed them to me, uncovered,
in the name of a Gordian slipknot,
begging for this Alexander's Sword.

Lock away your obsessions
in the vault of dreams, an iron box
hidden under your bed with the poems
you never shared, under shadowed locks.

Do not answer the knock of age,
when calls your summoned prince, his fate
in your arms obscured by cold fear
not warm desire. held at the gate.

the flavour of time

Deep draught drinks from the well of experience
have given me new perspectives on life and love and veiled
promises made in the name of lust and redemption.
the flavour of time can taint the desires that paled
in the deserts of loveless meanderings, the sense
of hunger revealed to the lost souls, thirsts unveiled
in the heart of the lover denied. prideful invention
covering for a hollow heart. bridges unbuilt. oceans unsailed.

the gypsy moth

A homeless heart, at night,
drawn to the flame eternal.
drawn to the lust infernal.
drawn to a dream nocturnal.
drawn to a need internal.
a beauty, bared in flight.

mirror within my mind

I see, within my mind, a mirror cold
and elegant. an infinitely reflective
surface, it's purpose to keep me sane
in the tempests of my soul and bold
emotions. to aid me in perspective
to this world, to show me the stain
of my sins and the shadow of hope.
imagine my surprise in staring in long
supplication of truth, praying for grace
and a heart of gold. the savage slope
of Sisyphus before me, but my will strong
and resolute. and to see your lovely face.

William F. DeVault

Cycle Two: Invocation

a taste of brimstone

I imagine your kiss. a simple taste of brimstone
on an angel's wing. it brings me to the edge of evil
intent. unspent thirst for your vitality will hone
my poet's tooth to a nosferatu's edge, but I will
not use it until the night when you are reconciled
that this sulphur is the air that you would breathe
for the rest of your life. I have never once defiled
the innocent and will not set your heart to grieve.

soft arms

Held out to me in a welcoming
 warmth. an invitation to dare
  challenge the world in a thundering
   wave of light. and if I care
to slip soft bandage to set
 my place in that embrace, then I
  must trust that this holy bet
   must be secured, until I die.

homeless heart

in the end, all hearts are homeless. cut away
from the pack by our own follies, loving perhaps
the wrong people or for the wrong reasons or
even to an inappropriate depth, considering our
need to parity. our need for completeness that caps
our very existence like twilight ends the day.

Edward bares his soul

he stares at me with button eyes and expressionless
shock and incredulity. he guarded well the gates
of youth, sprung at the touch of the heart's thief, gold
taken in the name of love. sad and passionless,
he sits on the weathered shelf, his presence states
his disapproval. an act observed, a tale untold.

The taste of blood

feral hunger. shared. dared. we cared to try
the wire over the fire that consumes so many,
a penny's worth of grace. that's all it takes.
and as the fakir plays his mesmeric tune, the snakes
consider our predicament and our pride. anyone
could have told us what we faced. but not why.

softer than skin

your heart in my hands. golden bands can not replace
the bondage of the soul. take the dream you carry, marry
it to your reason. in a season of dreams you will trace
the last of my supplications. leave now, or tarry
at your own risk. I will not usurp your will, base
iron over gold is not my way. be ready to run, be wary.

eternal kiss

the other night (in a distant reality
shared only in our minds and thus concealed)
our lips met. wet and warm. passionately
and shyly. and the truth was revealed.

William F. DeVault

Cycle Three: Memory's Shores

venom of time

knowing what we know, our hearts must now contend
with the venom of time. a cunning toxin that bends
your heart and mind in poisoned suffering, as lies
you tell yourself to resist the truth that denies
us the dignity of separation,
propels us towards bitter desolation.

glycerin tears

the light reflects off glycerin tears in a different way,
showing them false saline and proving the perfidy
of the false suitor's claims of passion and ardor.

test the steel. dare a kiss from the idols of the day,
where the light may cut and the fire may stir memory
of a dream you once had of what waits beyond the door.

that door. the one you erected to reinforce what you say
in the face of my suit to be the elect of your heart's giddy
empire. a fair hearing is all I want. nothing less, nothing more.

a world of challenges

this is not a place for cowards. the wounded bleed
but still need to march on, defending their peace
with a passion palpable and capable of playing seed
to the prayers of the coming generations. release
the dogs of hope and follow them, on foot if you must,
through the dark fens of our despairs and trace
their baying cries in the darkest shadows, though the dust
of the grave near blinds you. I'll share with you this race.

the gem of fire

more precious than a stone of the first water,
one where every seam and fracture
goes to give the gem greater brilliance.
catching the light, even in the dark dance
of denial and sorrow long swept
from the porches of your tears.
tears wept in memories that have crept
into your world. beauty only pain makes clear.

goldenheart by twilight

she stands, at the window. watching the velvet night
descend over fields of crisp snow, smoothing the fields
of trampled grass and broken glass that steal the light
until they serve as canvas to the frost of time. it yields
a peace within her, burning and strangely serene. she knows
the trail that lies before her, but the goldenheart must laugh
in strange irony. for she has ridden the savage blows
of time and sorrow to face her paramour. on a cryptic path.

bracing for Ragnarok

here. here, I say. we make our stand on these rocks.
no time to seek the higher ground. the sound of doom
now echoes in the halls of man and god together.
draw whatever tool of war you favor and wait with me.

the curse is sprung. I am undone and, like Thor mocks
the midgaard serpent to strike again, I must soon
challenge the edge of my legend and strain the tether
on the traces of my hawksfoot. please, wait with me.

for only I must face this wind, and I shall shield you
from the tempest which blows like an arrogant poet,
loud and epic, but only impactive if you linger. listen.
accept the glistening words as those of the soul's priest.

here, in this place a thousand lives from where new
dreams are formed, we have warmed our hearts and show it
in our eyes. I will remain, and the pain will fade again.
to be reborn when next I hear your voice. regret released.

autumnal

it is not yet winter, and yet you fear the cold.
the leaves are bright and brazen, highlights of bold
and newborn dreams of coming rebirth. flecks of red
and gold and brown and raging purple in the bed
of the forest giants. I am not there, my heart
is not that of a fading dream, but of a raging upstart
minotaur. stubborn and proud and full of fire and life.
I am not death, but a quickening proved on the season's knife.

Cycle Four: Dreams of the Damned

nightmare

alone. trapped by circumstance
outside the dance. the lover's knot
denied, my heart of gold, cold chance
betraying me. melting in the hot
embrace of runaway heart and pain.
a rain of saline. illusions of control
shown impotent. and against the grain
is to use the power of the poet's soul.

wet dream

I dreamed of you, last night.
images primitive and passionate.
flooding my sense with your essence, bright
and plutonic. gentle emotion cast to fate
as I took my fill of my desires, awakened
by a gentle voice and a sensuous fantasy
you shared with me once, when beckoned
to the edge of temptation by your beauty.

dream of falling

slow motion. I'm used to seeing this from the other side,
picking up the pieces of a shattered life and, with tube
of cyanoacrylate in hand, building a semblance of a friend.
maybe not what he or she was, but certainly enough to pride
myself on my jigsaw skills. but the ground now exudes
a certain Newtonian charm and it is my sudden end
I am about to witness. all for the want of never saying
what was in my heart. love unexpressed in anvil wings.

the second nightmare

it will not work, she says to me.
my response is to ask if being free
is all she needs, or if there is something
I can offer to reconcile my aching
soul to her fears. and her eyes moisten
as she speaks in inarticulate poison
given to her by a thousand past lies
told by false lovers. and all hope dies.

waking dream

I answered the phone and there you were.
reality reflected in a laugh, a sweet voice
evoking ten thousand prayers I dare not share
with God, for they are dark and full of lust.
and we talked to a while, as I sat in turn
both happy and sad. images flooding as noise
to the exchange. soft lover's kiss. your hair
against me as you slumber in my arms, in trust
that I am there out of love and true affection.
and I drift on these shadows in our conversation.

sleepwalker

tonight you will see me in your dreams.
I know you have seen me there before, you
have admitted as much. but tonight, it seems,
the fantasy will not be just a memory through
an illusion, but real in my heart. for I will
walk the winds of your soul to be there, alone,
to talk with you, or hold you, or share a real
moment before the sun dispels my desire's clone.

daydream

a simple house. a yard of green and gold and white
fencing, keeping our children, in their play, safe. you
are there, your hair rippling like wildflowers in the breeze
of a virgin continent. the one we made our own, bright
and beautiful. the smell of coming rain, the placid blue
of a sky that frames you like a rainbow in the trees.

William F. DeVault

Cycle Five: the Cold Illusions

second chances

It wasn't a mistake at the time. or at least
it didn't seem to be. and now, shackled by past actions,
I find myself forfeit to the darkness, the feast
of hope will pass me by, to die in loveless misdirections.

virtue and vice

we roll the cosmic dice.
hoping for some understanding.
reasoning virtue and vice.
requests revert to dark demanding.

passion pales before our prayers.
dreams of love and fears of falling
into emotion that cuts and burns and tears
wounds into our hearts. tenderness left wanting.

a little warmth

playing it safe leads to the darkest of disasters.
conservative actions out of cowardice are predestined
to come back against you and mock the masters
of your heart and mind and soul and flesh. the wind
is not always merciful, but love is always a risk,
a gamble. those who never learn the odds lose all.
a little warmth is meaningless in December's brisk
and unforgiving wind. mine is not a tepid call.

bartering truth

what is, is meaningless.   give the word and I will turn
an infinite number of realities on their ears and make
a kingdom of your heart. no sport of me, make you, burn
instead the fuel you have stored in sadness and rage, take
you passions and unleash them. seize your destiny and learn
the language of love from one for whom your flesh aches.

golden hearts by the pound

pyrite filings, pounded into tri-ventricled icons.
not to be confounded, I expounded on the virtues
of a goldenheart. an ancient dream of mine, a song
of my youth. and yes, I have kept searching, bruise
by bruise, cut by cut, scar for scar, I wear my prayer
as well as I can. the centaur dances, then romances
not out of pattern, but out of recognition. truthsayer,
soothsayer and love's labor not lost on false chances.

reflections on a wind forced by the passage of time

were I a younger man, my span nearer your own, perhaps
you would accept my suit at a moment's consideration.
but this is a different sphere, and here, your heart's clasp
is locked against these fingers, a restless vindication
is meaningless if not seen relevant to the case at hand
and I run risk of being judge unfit by prejudgement.
what words will wash away each sandblown band
of measured, pleasured time made before the present?

leap of faith

love without risk is not love. it is safety.
it is security. an allegory
sold in Hollywood to prevent a happy
ending anywhere except on the TV.

William F. DeVault

Cycle Six: the Delta

soft

a kiss. the core of eroticism. an entrapping
web, woven of soft, sensuous lips. barely brushing
to send a message of Promethian fire coruscating
through your writhing soul. face cupped in hands
reverent and strong. longing. all the thronging
emotions and unspent currencies of devotions
made to gods in the name of your flesh. to kiss.
to touch your soul in the guise of a martyred love.
rapture in a ravenwing dream. the scent of your
skin, the rustling of your breath on my face.
a growing zephyr of soft, pulsing warmth.

warm

you make your stand,
your hand steadying
your form against
the warm electric surges
that render you a
marionette
on my tongue.
dancing in pleasure,
embracing a treasure
of newfound ecstasy.

the creeping flush
like a gambler's hand
played in a warm pool
of a ready partner,
aces and nines,
impaled on the tines
of a soulmetal fork.
talking the talk.
walking the walk.
riding the ride
of a warm and sweet slide.

willing

if I were born a woman, I would still lust for you.
I would seek to steal your will and then bid you ignore
the attentions of the young men, instead taking
you into my bed, to pleasure you a thousand new
and erotic ways. your taste on my tongue. the roar
of blood in your veins made deafening in waking
to the touch of my flesh. silks of green and blue,
sliding sensuously across your soft breasts, more
sinfully sweet than any man's lies. our thirsts slaking.

wet

I read you my poetry and you sat, unmoving.
unfeeling. seemingly untouched by the words I spun
in gossamer entreaty to your heart and mind and sex.
but I saw, in your eyes, that between your thighs, I bring
out the moisture of your aching flesh. and for one
infinite instant, I saw the walls collapse in reflex
passion. you did not speak. you did not need to.
I saw. and I knelt before you and gently kissed
your delicate hands. feeling the tension flowing
like the wetness you crossed your legs to dam, true
to your resistance. I bent and softly, suddenly, placed
my lips at the very hem of your dress and in a knowing
kiss, lit a fire that spread like the red blossom
that traced its way across your warm flesh and awoke
the tigers in your souls. hungry and playful.
I did not stop there. I boldly traced your bosom
with a hundred kisses as you fought the fire, but never spoke
a single word to stop what happened next. sweet and sinful.

gentle feast

softer than any mere marinated dish
served by any chef. your sweet, warm flesh
tastes like life itself, held on a shelf
called fear nearly too long. I claim
this for my last repast, one that will last
all the days of my life. if you will it.

chosen voices

you close your eyes and hear gentle entreaties,
urging on your hands, damp with your heart's dew.
illusory lovers, fed by your stored passions, sweetly
they pleasure you. and I would like if I were one, too.

impalement

like taking saddle on a new mount
you do not know what to expect, fully.
experience is an illusion as you count
a thousand reasons not to do this, reality
is setting in and it looks like it may be more
than you bargained for, more than you are ready for.

but the desire to try this mount is real.
and you can feel the need to bleed your soul
for this transfusion of desire. you steal
a final look and guide your flesh to seize control
of my pleasure, of my measure.

Cycle Seven: Consummation and Beyond

commitment

I will not take, in any sense,
you or your love, if not convinced
that the barter, for you, represents
an honest advantage. promised
and kept by a man who wishes
to give you more than a rogue's kisses.

ancient skies

I wonder if, ten thousand years ago, a man
much like me, looked with pride on his bride,
as I do you this day. I am swept away by an
inarticulate joy. barely able to answer when called,
barely able to recall anything but the sense of joy
I felt when you assented first to this simple ceremony.

new life

between us. a new bond.
a life is spawned
in eloquent announcement
of our shared passion.
we will fashion
a new tapesty in the time spent
giving our love in a thousand ways.
giving our love in a thousand ways.

the peasant blouse

we hid, in the bus stop, until the rain stopped.
but by then, watching the way that wet peasant blouse
clung to you, I was in no hurry to leave and you,
having seen my regarding stare, were busy in my arms,
sharing your warmth with me, as I shared my opinion
of your beauty in small sighs. and gentle kisses.

security

I offered my heart, my life, my home, my name.
and these I will never take away.
I give you my dreams, my prayers, my hopes, my strength.
and this is enough, I pray.

the centaur's home in a golden heart

I found you. and, by your will, I will keep you
deep and soulbound, within my reality.
I owe you my trust, my faith, my love and you
owe me nothing in return. it is freely
given. for I would make my home in the true
goldenheart, which I have found. happy
am I to have found you. and there are few
who find such treasure or pleasure as we
can if you would but trust this love, new
it is to your understanding, but beauty
is its core and for such peace we both are due.

bare feet on a wooden floor

I ate a daisy today. (to settle a bet between my child
and my wife if I could or would.) Daddy is not so ancient
that he has forgotten the value of play in the lurking wild
of a newly discovered world. Mommy has been patient,
but loves and lives for and with this world, and late
at night, while our children sleep, goes on a date
with me in the kitchen, dancing strange emotions stored
in cookie jar hearts that never break. bare feet on a wooden floor.

About the author

William F. DeVault started writing poetry at the tender age of 8, but it was not until 17, when he discovered the profound impact his words could have on people, that he came of age as a writer and began to take it seriously, putting aside a path designed to enter the ministry.

With the dissemination of his "Panther Cycles" on the internet in 1995-1996, and "The Goldenheart Cycles" in late 1995, his following built to a worldwide status and in September of 1996, when he launched his first website "The City of Legends", Yahoo granted him the sobriquet of the Romantic Poet of the Internet.

Twice married and divorced, with three children from his first marriage, he is, at this writing, focusing on his writing and collecting his existing works.

Born in Greenville, South Carolina, raised all over the United States, he counts Venice Beach California as his home.

www.ingramcontent.com/pod-product-compliance
Lightning Source LLC
Chambersburg PA
CBHW061508040426
42450CB00008B/1528